THE
SOUTHAMPTON
FOOTBALL CLUB
ANNUAL 2017

Written by Tom Biggs and Gordon Simpson

Design by Duncan Cook Drummond

A Grange Publication

©2016. Published by Grange Communications Ltd.,
Edinburgh, under licence from Southampton Football Club.
Printed in the EU.

Photographs © Matt Watson, Naomi Baker
and Michael Jones

ISBN 978-1-911287-14-8

CONTENTS

Welcome to the Official
Southampton
Football Club
Annual 2017!

Over the next 60 pages there are plenty of fantastic features for Southampton fans of all ages to enjoy, whether you're just starting out as a Saints supporter or you've got red and white stripes running through you!

We kick off with a review of what proved to be another record-breaking season for the club, as Saints amassed an impressive 63 points in the Premier League to ensure themselves a sixth-placed finish and European football for the current campaign!

There's a look back at some of the best goals, games and saves from the 2015/16 season, while we run you through Kelvin Davis's testimonial and the club's prestigious awards night.

We'll also introduce you to all of Saints' summer signings – including the new manager – making sure you know all you need to about the current team for the 2016/17 campaign.

Also included are some healthy eating tips from the club's chef, while Head of Sports Science Alek Gross has some great advice for you.

That's not all – we've got a big quiz and plenty of puzzlers for you to put your Saints knowledge to the test!

Enjoy your read, Saints fans!

SEASON
OVERVIEW
2015/16

Southampton's record-breaking 2014/15 season was always going to be difficult to top – but that didn't stop the team doing just that!

The 2015/16 campaign proved to be the club's most incredible Premier League season yet, as they produced both their highest ever finish – sixth – and greatest ever points total – 63 – in the competition.

There were many wonderful memories along the way, with Saints recording wins against Manchester United, Manchester City, Chelsea, Tottenham, Arsenal and Liverpool at various points.

Fraser Forster also returned from a long-term knee injury to set a club record for the longest run of minutes without conceding, while the campaign ended in spectacular fashion as the team secured qualification to the Europa League group stages.

Here we relive all the great memories of a season to treasure…

JULY/AUGUST

While most other clubs were still working through their pre-season schedules, Southampton's campaign had already begun in earnest with their Europa League qualifier against Vitesse.

On a memorable night at St Mary's, Saints ended a 34-year wait for a win in Europe, as they cruised past the Dutch club 3-0, thanks to goals from Graziano Pellè, Dušan Tadić and Shane Long.

Saints finished the job a week later with a 2-0 win in Arnhem, with Pellè and Sadio Mané scoring, before attention turned to the start of the Premier League season.

They started with a 2-2 draw at Newcastle, with Pellè again on target, while Long's late header rescued a point. However, the positive start came to a halt when Saints returned home, as they were comfortably beaten 3-0 by Everton.

The frustration then continued, as Saints drew 1-1 at home to Danish champions FC Midtjylland in the first leg of their Europa League play-off, and the heartbreak was complete a week later, as they lost 1-0 in the away leg to fall just short of the group stages.

In between, the team had drawn 0-0 at newly-promoted Watford, but they responded well in their final match of the month, beating Norwich 3-0 at St Mary's, with Pellè setting them on the way, before Tadić scored twice after half time.

SEPTEMBER

September started in encouraging fashion for the club, as they completed the signing of long-term target Virgil van Dijk, with the Dutch centre-back joining from Celtic.

Van Dijk impressed on his debut, with his assured performance at the heart of defence proving the highlight of an otherwise dour 0-0 draw at West Brom.

If that game had lacked excitement, Saints' next one certainly didn't, as they were cruelly beaten 3-2 at home by Manchester United. Despite dominating for large spells and leading through Graziano Pellè, who also added a second later on, they were beaten by two strikes from Anthony Martial and a Juan Mata effort.

Still, the team were showing positive signs and they continued to do so with a 6-0 win at MK Dons in the third round of the Capital One Cup – having received a bye through the second round due to their involvement in Europe.

Jay Rodriguez, who produced a goal-of-the-season contender by beating a few players at speed and curling a shot inside the far corner, scored twice, as did Sadio Mané and Shane Long.

It proved to be an important result, kick-starting an eight-match unbeaten streak, with the next game producing a 3-1 win over Swansea in the Premier League. Van Dijk scored his first goal for the club, while a Ki Sung-Yeung own-goal and a Mané effort completed the victory.

OCTOBER

Southampton's momentum was building by this point, but many might have expected it to come to a halt when they visited defending champions Chelsea.

That would not be the case though, as they produced one of their finest results of the season, triumphing 3-1 for a first victory at Stamford Bridge since 2002.

Saints had trailed to an early Willian free-kick, but Steven Davis' crisp low strike from 20-yards brought them level just before half time. They then demolished the Blues after the break, with Sadio Mané being played through to finish, before Graziano Pellè produced a brilliant strike across goal on the counter for the third.

After a short break for international duty, Saints were next in action at home to Leicester City. Goals from José Fonte and Virgil van Dijk put them firmly in command, but the Foxes stormed back after half time with two goals from Jamie Vardy to snatch a draw.

Saints would come from behind away from home themselves in their next game, as a scrambled effort from Mané, who would also be sent off late on for two bookings, earned a 1-1 draw at Liverpool.

October then came to a close with a 2-1 home win over Aston Villa that booked a place in the Capital One Cup quarter-finals, as Maya Yoshida scored a spectacular strike, while Pellè finished off an impressive team move for the decisive goal.

NOVEMBER

A first ever top-flight clash with newly-promoted Bournemouth kicked off this month, and Saints ensured their status as the area's dominant club remained firmly intact.

Their 2-0 victory came via a side-footed Steven Davis effort from a Ryan Bertrand cross, before Graziano Pellè headed home a Dušan Tadić delivery.

The team would then extend its unbeaten run to eight matches with a 1-0 victory away to Sunderland that moved them to within a point of the Premier League's top five.

Saints dominated the match, but had to wait for the 69th minute to get the decisive breakthrough, as Tadić calmly stroked home a penalty after Yann M'Vila had tripped Bertrand, ending a 12-year wait for a win at the Stadium of Light.

Again though, an international break came at the wrong time, as form dipped alarmingly when the team returned to action.

A closely contested home game with Stoke City went the way of the visitors, thanks to an early near-post finish from Bojan Krkić, before the side made the trip to Manchester City.

It proved to be another frustrating day, as Kevin de Bruyne gave the hosts an early lead, while they doubled their advantage through a deflected effort from Fabian Delph.

Saints restored hope after half time, as Shane Long headed in a Sadio Mané cross, but Aleksandar Kolarov ended the prospect of a comeback by netting City's third.

DECEMBER

The run-up to Christmas is meant to be a time of cheer, but it was anything but for Southampton.

December began ominously, with a 6-1 humbling at home to Liverpool in the quarter-finals of the Capital One Cup.

Sadio Mané had headed Saints in front inside the first minute but things quickly unravelled, with Daniel Sturridge scoring two quick-fire goals, ahead of Divock Origi netting a hat-trick and Jordan Ibe adding another.

With confidence low, it then took a late Oriol Romeu goal to rescue a point against rock-bottom Aston Villa at St Mary's, as the side got back to Premier League action.

A 1-0 defeat at Crystal Palace followed, before a 2-0 home loss against Tottenham Hotspur and former manager Mauricio Pochettino.

Fortunately though, Boxing Day brought a much needed lifting of spirits as Saints produced a sensational performance to thump Arsenal 4-0 at home – Cuco Martina setting them on the way with his swerving, long-range wonder strike, while Shane Long scored twice either side of a José Fonte goal.

It looked as though the result had snapped the team out of its funk, as they swarmed over West Ham at the Boleyn Ground two days later.

But they were punished for scoring only once – via an early Carl Jenkinson own goal – as West Ham turned the game on its head after half time to win 2-1 through ex-Saint Michail Antonio and Andy Carroll.

JANUARY

If Saints were hoping for the new year to bring a new start, they were to be disappointed.

The poor form continued as they were beaten 1-0 by Norwich City at Carrow Road, with Alex Tettey's superb late strike coming shortly after Victor Wanyama had been sent off for a second yellow card.

Saints then returned home for an FA Cup clash with Crystal Palace but, for the second season running, were dumped out of the competition by the Eagles at St Mary's, with Joel Ward and Wilfried Zaha scoring either side of an Oriol Romeu equaliser.

The bad run ended there though, as a Shane Long header and a Dušan Tadić strike earned a 2-0 home win over Watford – a game that also marked the return of goalkeeper Fraser Forster after ten months out with a knee injury.

The good news continued as Saints completed the signing of striker Charlie Austin from QPR on the same day they beat West Brom 3-0 at St Mary's – James Ward-Prowse netting a brilliant 25-yard free-kick, followed by a penalty, before Tadić scored the third.

The best of the month was still to come though, as the team went to Old Trafford and won for the second season in succession.

Austin's signing paid instant dividends as he came off the bench late on for his debut, meeting a Ward-Prowse free-kick in the 87th minute to head home and give the visitors another treasured 1-0 win.

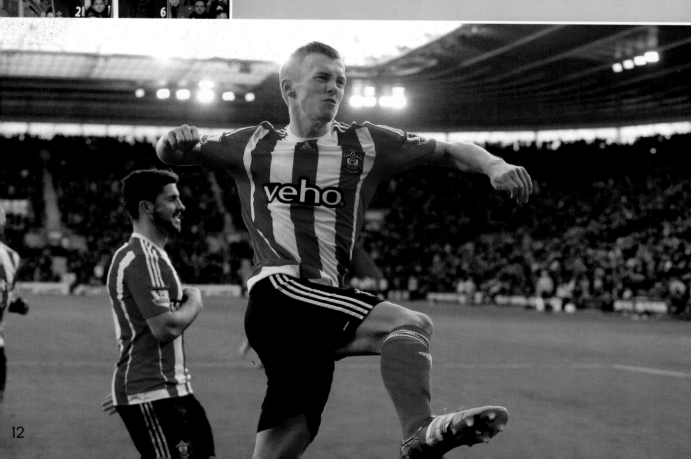

FEBRUARY

Sometimes in football, a 0-0 draw can prove just as exciting or dramatic as a game filled with goals.

Saints' trip to Arsenal at the start of February was just such an occasion, as goalkeeper Fraser Forster produced a display that will live long in the memory.

Time and time again, the England international – who had kept three clean sheets coming into this game after returning from injury – denied the Gunners' attack, as the visitors secured a precious point to extend their unbeaten run to four matches.

A 1-0 home win over fellow European chasers West Ham followed, with Maya Yoshida netting the decisive effort from close range. The only sour note was another red card for Victor Wanyama, resulting in a five-match ban for the midfielder.

Saints didn't let that affect them though, as they made it six games unbeaten – and six clean sheets in succession – with a 1-0 victory at Swansea, as Shane Long headed a late winner.

Forster would then beat Paul Jones' record for the longest run of top-flight minutes without conceding, but his streak ended at 708 minutes at home to Chelsea, as a late Cesc Fàbregas cross eluded everyone and found the bottom corner to cancel out Long's opener.

Sadly for Saints, Chelsea still had time to find a winner, through Branislav Ivanović's thumping header from an added-time corner. Still, Forster would be recognised for his form with the Premier League Player of the Month award.

MARCH

Southampton had played well enough against Chelsea that their confidence should not have been dented, but they were far from their best when they visited Bournemouth at the start of this month.

Headers from Steve Cook and Benik Afobe gave the home side a deserved 2-0 win, as Saints remained seventh but lost ground on the teams above.

A disappointing 1-1 home draw with relegation-threatened Sunderland would follow, although it could have been far worse, with Virgil van Dijk's effort deep into added time cancelling out Jermain Defoe's opener.

Having slipped to ninth, Saints were in need of a win to re-energise their European hopes when they travelled to Stoke, and they got it with a pair of Graziano Pellè goals in the first-half at Britannia Stadium – enough to earn a 2-1 victory.

A better result followed a week later, as the team produced a famous comeback to beat Liverpool 3-2 at St Mary's.

Early goals from Philippe Coutinho and Daniel Sturridge made for an ominous start, with echoes of the 6-1 League Cup win earlier in the season, and when Sadio Mané had a second-half penalty saved it looked like there would be only one outcome.

But Mané's pass was brilliant finish across goal from a Pellè followed by the Italian striker lashing in a stunning equaliser from 20-yards. Pellè then turned provider again, slipping in Mané to complete a most incredible rally.

APRIL

The end of another international break coincided with another disappointing result, as Southampton lost 1-0 to a Leicester City side who would go on to win the most unlikely of Premier League titles.

Saints were unfortunate not to lead in the early stages, as Sadio Mané went through and rounded the 'keeper with his shot hitting the arm of Danny Simpson, only for no penalty to be awarded.

Wes Morgan's header later in the half condemned the visitors to a cruel defeat, but they responded emphatically in their next match as they brushed Newcastle aside 3-1 at St Mary's, with Shane Long, Graziano Pellè and Victor Wanyama all on target.

Saints then travelled to a struggling Everton, but required a late Mané goal to earn a draw after Ramiro Funes Mori had put the hosts in front.

It would prove to be the team's last dropped points of the season, as they embarked on a sensational run of form to end the campaign.

That started with their last game in April, as they won 4-2 against an already-relegated Aston Villa team.

Shane Long headed Saints in front, before Dušan Tadić made it 2-0. Ashley Westwood got one back for the hosts ahead of half time, but Tadić made it 3-1 after the break.

After another Westwood goal, Mané's late header ensured the visitors took a deserved three points.

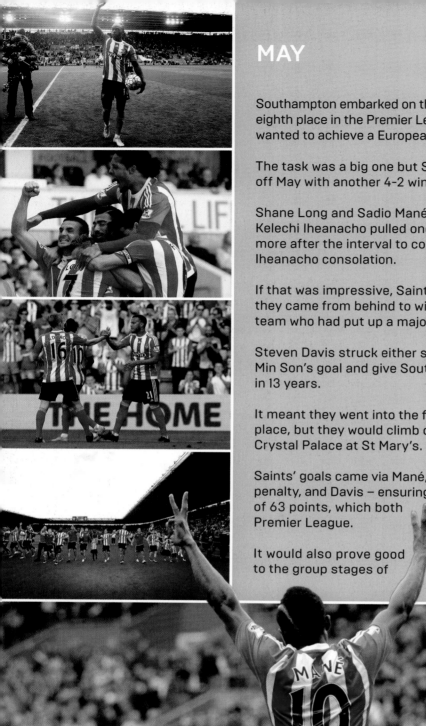

MAY

Southampton embarked on their final three matches of the season in eighth place in the Premier League and with no margin for error if they wanted to achieve a European spot for a second successive season.

The task was a big one but Saints were more than up to it, kicking off May with another 4-2 win, this time at home to Manchester City.

Shane Long and Sadio Mané put the hosts 2-0 ahead and, although Kelechi Iheanacho pulled one back on half time, Mané struck twice more after the interval to complete his hat-trick, ahead of another Iheanacho consolation.

If that was impressive, Saints' next game was even more so, as they came from behind to win 2-1 against a Tottenham Hotspur team who had put up a major title challenge.

Steven Davis struck either side of the interval to overcome Heung-Min Son's goal and give Southampton a first win at White Hart Lane in 13 years.

It meant they went into the final game of the season in seventh place, but they would climb one spot higher with a 4-1 thumping of Crystal Palace at St Mary's.

Saints' goals came via Mané, Graziano Pellè, a Ryan Bertrand penalty, and Davis – ensuring a sixth-place finish and a final total of 63 points, which both represented club records in the Premier League.

It would also prove good enough for automatic qualification to the group stages of the Europa League.

BEHIND-THE-SCENES
PHOTOS

You're blocking the view, José!

A fantastic season means loads of fantastic photos! Here we take a look at some of the behind-the-scenes images you may have missed from Saints' remarkable 2015/16 campaign.

Looking sharp, Virgil!

We can see you, Kelvin!

Davo's delight in training.

Thumbs up from Fraser.

A legend watches on.

That's not your camera, Matt.

Careful Maya, don't drop it!

At home with Cuco.

Prowsey poses for the camera.

What's so funny, Ryan?

Meet Alfie, the Staplewood cat!

Celebrations on a plane.

2015/16
AWARD WINNERS

After José Fonte had done the double following an impressive 2014/15 campaign, another defender repeated the feat the following season, as Virgil van Dijk was the big winner at the club's end-of-season Player Awards night.

GARMIN PLAYERS' PLAYER OF THE SEASON:
VIRGIL VAN DIJK

SOLENT UNIVERSITY YOUNG PLAYER OF THE SEASON:
ALFIE JONES

A summer signing from Celtic, Virgil van Dijk made an immediate impression as he put on an excellent display in a goalless draw at West Bromwich Albion. His form continued over the course of the season, as he picked up two Player of the Month awards and a league nomination. He finished ahead of striker Shane Long and midfielder Steven Davis to be named by his teammates as the club's best player of 2015/16.

Van Dijk said: "From the first day I came here I felt very welcomed. I think all the lads in the group have been amazing as well and I think the team is perfect. I'm very grateful for everything since I came here."

Defender Alfie Jones was named as the club's Young Player of the Season, as his excellent form for Saints' Under-18s and Under-21s was rewarded. Jones began the season with Craig Fleming's Under-18s, but made the step up to Martin Hunter's development side after Christmas and never looked back. He was even called up to train with the first team on a number of occasions.

Jones said: "It's unbelievable and it's a massive honour for me. It has been a good year. It was a tough one for me, but it was just an amazing experience and to get this tops it all off."

PRESIDENT'S CHOICE AWARD:
RYAN BERTRAND

OCTA FX FANS' PLAYER OF THE SEASON:
VIRGIL VAN DIJK

On a night dominated by defenders, it was Ryan Bertrand who was presented with the President's Choice award by Honorary President Terry Paine MBE. Bertrand made a big impression over the course of the season, as he featured at centre-back, left-back and wing-back to help Saints achieve another record-breaking finish.

"I wasn't expecting to win anything", Bertrand said. "To be honest, with the awards up for grabs, it slipped my mind how prestigious this award is. I had a brief reminder of that and it's an honour to win it. I'm very thankful."

Virgil van Dijk completed the double, as he collected the big award of the night – Fans' Player of the Season 2015/16. Having already won the Players' Player award, van Dijk was voted by fans as the club's top performer over the course of the 2015/16 season. The defender finished ahead of Shane Long and Steven Davis once again.

"I want to thank everyone who voted for me, of course", van Dijk said. "There are no words for this. I'm just very happy. I think the fans have been amazing for me this year and hopefully we can continue that way."

RADIO TAXIS GOAL OF THE SEASON:
CUCO MARTINA VS ARSENAL (H)

LONG SERVICE AWARD:
KELVIN DAVIS

There were some great goals scored by Saints over the course of the 2015/16 season, but there was only ever going to be one winner. Cuco Martina's stunning strike against Arsenal in the 4-0 win on Boxing Day was voted as the best – receiving over 80 per cent of the votes. The Curaçao international, who was making his full Premier League debut, fired home brilliantly against the Gunners to set Saints on their way to a memorable win.

The final award of the night was presented to long-serving goalkeeper Kelvin Davis, thanking him for his excellent service to Saints. Having joined in 2006, Davis went on to make over 300 appearances for the club in all competitions, achieving back-to-back promotions and playing a key role in Saints' remarkable rise. The goalkeeper was presented with a special watch by his teammates – although he said he wasn't sure on the colour!

SAINTS' REMARKABLE RISE

Since relegation from the Championship in 2009, Southampton have enjoyed a remarkable rise, achieving continued success over the course of seven seasons. Here we take a look back at Saints' incredible progression.

2009/10

A ten-point deduction was always going to make it tough for Alan Pardew's Saints, but with Markus Liebherr becoming owner and a number of key signings made, they enjoyed a positive season. A seventh-placed finish in League 1 – missing out on the play-offs by just one place – and success at Wembley in the Johnstone's Paint Trophy final against Carlisle meant spirits were high again at St Mary's.

2010/11

The 2010/11 season marked Saints' 125th anniversary and the players, under new manager Nigel Adkins who was appointed in September 2010, didn't disappoint. A remarkable run towards the end of the season, in which Saints lost just one of their last 15 games, saw Adkins' men finish the season in second – ensuring they would be back in the Championship for the following campaign.

2011/12

Confidence was high at St Mary's as the new season got under way, but few could have

predicted just how successful it would prove to be for Saints. Nigel Adkins' men never dropped out of the top two over the course of the campaign, eventually finishing a point behind champions Reading to seal back-to-back promotions and a return to the top flight of English football.

2012/13

After a seven-year absence, Nigel Adkins quickly set about ensuring Saints would be competitive in the Premier League. Sitting just outside the relegation zone in mid-January, Adkins was replaced

by Mauricio Pochettino, who continued the club's upward trajectory by finishing 14th in the table come the end of the campaign. Excellent wins against Manchester City, Chelsea and Liverpool showed just how far Saints had come.

2013/14

Saints were now going in search of a fifth straight season of progression, and under Mauricio Pochettino they

didn't disappoint. The likes of Adam Lallana, Rickie Lambert and Morgan Schneiderlin –

who had been there since the League 1 days – were key members of a side that sat third in the table after 11 games. Saints would eventually finish eighth in the table thanks to a four-game unbeaten run at the end of the campaign.

2014/15

After Mauricio Pochettino's departure, it was now down to Ronald Koeman to continue Saints' progression. The Dutchman enjoyed a hugely

successful start to his first season in charge, with Saints in a Champions League spot up until February. A tough

second half of the campaign meant they couldn't stay in the top four, but they finished

in seventh and in the process sealed a UEFA Europa League spot for the following season.

2015/16

Fourteenth. Eighth. Seventh. Could Saints improve again in the Premier League? Under Ronald Koeman that's exactly what they did. Saints found the going tough at the start of the season, and were knocked out of the UEFA Europa League in the play-off round, but they enjoyed a remarkable second half of the season. Saints picked up 39 points to finish sixth with a record-breaking points total of 63, and seal a spot in the Europa League group stages!

KELVIN'S BIG NIGHT

Kelvin Davis's Testimonial – 17 MAY 2016

ON A SPECIAL NIGHT at St Mary's, goalkeeper Kelvin Davis was rewarded for his terrific service to Southampton Football Club with a testimonial match.

The testimonial saw a current Saints XI take on a Promotions Eleven – a team made up of players who featured alongside Kelvin during the club's back-to-back promotions in 2011 and 2012.

Club legend Rickie Lambert, winger Jason Puncheon, midfielder Jack Cork and even current defender José Fonte lined up for the Promotions XI, with nearly 20,000 fans turning out to celebrate Kelvin and the club's success.

Supporters were treated to plenty of goals, but they'll have needed to be in their seats early – Kelvin scored the opening goal with the first kick of the game from the halfway line!

Graziano Pellè and Charlie Austin scored to put the current Saints side 2-1 up, but two goals from former winger Lee Holmes made it 3-2. Austin got his second to make it 3-3 at half time, before Harrison Reed restored the lead for the current Saints team.

Shane Long then made it 5-3 with 15 minutes to go, before Kelvin and his son Sonnie came on for opposite sides. After his dad had denied him with three good saves, Sonnie finally scored with the last kick of the game – smashing home a penalty that left Kelvin with no chance!

Speaking after his big night, Kelvin said: "Ten seasons and I'm proud of every minute. I know it's easy to say, but I respect every single fan for turning up, not just for me, but for the charity. I want to see this club go even further, I want to see us win trophies and I believe we can."

Liver and Pancreatic Cancer Research & Development Charity was Kelvin's chosen charity for his testimonial.

GOAL 1
Cuco Martina vs Arsenal (H)

This jaw-dropping strike deservedly won the club's Goal of the Season award. Martina's astonishing first-time hit from 30 yards started well outside the far post, but swerved perfectly to find the bottom corner.

GOAL 2
Jay Rodriguez vs MK Dons (A)

Starting just inside his own half, Rodriguez flicked the ball between two MK Dons players and sprinted past them, before cutting inside another defender and bending a glorious shot inside the far post from 18 yards.

GOAL 3
Steven Davis vs Chelsea (A)

What a strike! The midfielder showed incredible technique to lash a bouncing, spinning ball low and inside the near post from 20 yards, after Graziano Pellè had brilliantly chested down José Fonte's angled pass.

GOAL 4
Graziano Pellè vs Liverpool (H)

Pellè, who has a knack for a spectacular goal, capped off a neat move that also featured Steven Davis and Shane Long, as he shifted the ball onto his left foot 20 yards out and unleashed a cannon of a left-foot shot that flew into the far corner.

GOAL 5
James Ward-Prowse vs West Bromwich Albion (H)

Faced with a free-kick 25 yards out, almost in line with the left edge of the penalty area, Ward-Prowse hit a glorious effort that curled over the wall and dipped just under the bar to find the near top corner.

1 Southampton 3-2 Liverpool

There were so many options for the best game of the season, but this one was truly exceptional. Saints were 2-0 down, and Sadio Mané had missed a penalty, when they completed the most sensational comeback with Mané scoring twice and Graziano Pellè getting the equaliser in between.

2 Manchester United 0-1 Southampton

This might not have been the most exciting of games, or the biggest margin of victory, but Saints – for the second season in succession – secured a famous triumph at Old Trafford, as Charlie Austin came off the bench for a debut to remember, heading in the winner from James Ward-Prowse's 87th-minute pass.

3 Chelsea 1-3 Southampton

Surely it doesn't get much tougher than the defending champions away from home? Well, not for Saints, who made light work of Chelsea at Stamford Bridge. Willian gave the hosts the lead, but Saints levelled through Steven Davis, before Sadio Mané and Graziano Pellè completed the turnaround after half time.

4 Southampton 4-0 Arsenal

Saints hadn't won in six games coming into this Boxing Day clash, but you wouldn't have known it as they demolished the Gunners at St Mary's. Cuco Martina's wonder goal set them on the way, with José Fonte then scoring in between two Shane Long goals in the second half to complete the rout.

5 Southampton 4-2 Manchester City

Even this scoreline probably doesn't reflect quite how dominant Saints were. Shane Long and Sadio Mané each scored in the space of three first-half minutes to put the hosts in command. Kelechi Iheanacho pulled one back for City, but Mané ended any hopes of them coming back by completing his hat-trick with two second-half goals, ahead of Iheanacho adding another consolation late on.

1 Fraser Forster vs Arsenal

Forster produced one of the finest Saints goalkeeping displays in recent memory, and also a contender for the best save of the entire Premier League season, at Emirates Stadium. Hector Bellerin's cross was headed goalwards by Olivier Giroud, with Mesut Özil then diverting the ball from three yards out, only for Forster to stick out his left arm and deflect it inches wide.

2 Fraser Forster vs Leicester

Not only was this one of Forster's best saves of the season, but it was notable for the fact that it came from one of his teammates. Danny Drinkwater's dangerous, skidding ball from the right at King Power Stadium was accidentally sent looping towards the far top corner by a sliding José Fonte, only for Forster to readjust, fling himself backwards and somehow tip the ball away.

3 Fraser Forster vs West Ham

In a crucial game with fellow European rivals West Ham at St Mary's, Forster produced a stop of enormous importance. Saints were leading 1-0 when Dimitri Payet whipped in a free-kick from the left, with Winston Reid meeting it with a thumping header from close range, only for Forster to leap to his left and somehow palm the ball away to help the hosts to three big points.

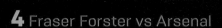

4 Fraser Forster vs Arsenal

Another one of many saves Forster made on the way to this incredible 0-0 at Emirates Stadium. Olivier Giroud's curling effort from 18 yards, after Aaron Ramsey had squared the ball to him, was arcing beautifully into the far top corner. However, it never made it, as Forster flung himself to his left, and made a jaw-dropping one-handed stop.

5 Fraser Forster vs Liverpool

Saints were already 2-0 down at St Mary's when Joe Allen was sent clear through on goal in the first half. He looked set to finish the game off, but his low strike was diverted behind brilliantly by Forster's right leg. How important was it? Saints ended up winning 3-2 and finishing three points above Liverpool at the end of the season.

SOUTHAMPTON goalkeeper **Fraser Forster** wrote himself into the club's record books during an incredible 2015/16 season.

Forster made a spectacular return from injury in January, going 708 minutes – or just shy of 12 hours – in the Premier League before conceding a goal.

That smashed the previous Saints record of 666 consecutive top-flight minutes without being beaten, which was set by Paul Jones in 2001.

Prior to his incredible run, Forster had been sidelined for ten months with a knee injury, which he suffered in a 2-0 home win over Burnley, in March 2015.

"I saw it as an opportunity to come back fitter and stronger than I'd ever been before," said Forster.

He wasn't wrong! His streak began with his appearance in a 2-0 home win over Watford in January – a result that put the team's run of just one victory in ten matches behind them.

Forster's next clean sheet came in a 3-0 success over West Brom at St Mary's before he shut out Manchester United at Old Trafford, as Saints won there 1-0 for the second season in succession.

The England international's most memorable game of the whole run then came when the side travelled to Arsenal.

Forster produced save after stunning save to deny the Gunners, in what was a display that will live long in the memory, as Saints earned a valuable 0-0 draw.

His sensational form continued in the 1-0 home win over West Ham, making a number of other notable saves, before a sixth successive clean sheet arrived in another 1-0 victory, this time at Swansea.

He nearly tied another Jones record, of seven consecutive Premier League clean sheets in a row, before being beaten in the 78th minute of the home game against Chelsea, at the end of February, as a Cesc Fàbregas cross eluded everyone and ended up in the far corner.

Draw Sammy Saint

Saints Puzzlers

Can you find the 12 words associated with Saints in our word search? Words can go horizontally, vertically and diagonally.

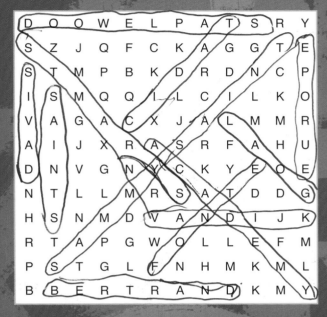

D	O	O	W	E	L	P	A	T	S	R	Y
S	Z	J	Q	F	C	K	A	G	G	T	E
S	T	M	P	B	K	D	R	D	N	C	P
I	S	M	Q	Q	I	L	C	I	L	K	O
V	A	G	A	C	X	J	A	L	M	M	R
A	I	J	X	R	A	S	R	F	A	H	U
D	N	V	G	N	Y	C	K	Y	E	O	E
N	T	L	L	M	R	S	A	T	D	D	G
H	S	N	M	D	V	A	N	D	I	J	K
R	T	A	P	G	W	O	L	L	E	F	M
P	S	T	G	L	F	N	H	M	K	M	L
B	B	E	R	T	R	A	N	D	K	M	Y

Davis
Fonte
Van Dijk
St Marys
Saints
Tadic

Staplewood
Goal
Europe
Sammy Saint
Bertrand
Academy

DOWN

1. Which Saints Academy graduate became the most expensive player in the world when he joined Real Madrid from Tottenham Hotspur?

4. What is the name of Saints' home ground?

5. What is the name of Saints' club mascot?

9. Which Saints player previously played for Reading, West Bromwich Albion and Hull City?

ACROSS

2. Cuco Martina plays his international football for which country?

3. Who is Saints' captain?

6. What is the club's nickname?

7. Which sports company makes Saints' home and away kits?

8. Which Saints player captained England Under-21s at the Toulon Tournament 2016?

10. Who scored Saints' last goal of the 2015/16 season?

11. What is Ryan Bertrand's squad number with Saints?

Answers on page 62/63.

Meet the New Boss

There's a new man in charge of Southampton this season. We've picked out five key facts about the club's new manager Claude Puel that you might not know – and definitely should!

1. France and Arsenal legend Thierry Henry credits Puel for the way in which he developed his famous finishing technique. While working alongside Puel at AS Monaco, Henry was made to rehearse the same sequence to shooting over and over again. After netting a goal against Ireland in Dublin to all but seal France's spot at the 2006 World Cup, Henry said: "I want to dedicate it to Claude Puel."

2. With Saints embarking on their maiden UEFA Europa League group stage campaign, Puel's European experience could well come in handy. The Frenchman has overseen 82 European games as a manager, winning 34 of those and drawing 25. He reached the semi-finals of the UEFA Champions League with Lyon in 2010.

3. Puel shares something in common with Saints legend Matt Le Tissier. The former defensive midfielder spent his entire playing career with AS Monaco – a spell spanning 17 seasons. Le Tissier did the same at Saints, spending 16 years with the club. Puel also had a spell as reserve manager and manager with the French outfit.

4. During his time in France, Puel handed senior debuts to a number of high-profile players. The likes of Eden Hazard, Eric Abidal, Hugo Lloris, Yohan Cabaye and Alexandre Lacazette have all benefited from Puel's willingness to give youth a chance, something Saints fans will be hoping to see more of following his arrival in England.

5. Puel enjoyed instant success as a manager. After joining Monaco in January 1999, he guided the club to the Ligue 1 title in his first full season. Their success in 2000 was the last time Monaco won the first division title in France. After winning it twice as a player, it was the third time in which Puel had tasted league success with Monaco.

Matt Le Tissier 1985 - 2002

FACTFILE:

Date of birth: 2nd September 1961

Place of birth: Castres, France

Height: 5ft 9in

Playing position: Defensive midfielder

Playing career: Monaco (1979-1996)

Teams managed: Monaco (1999-2001), Lille (2002-2008), Lyon (2008-2011), Nice (2012-2016)

Playing honours: Ligue 1 (1982, 1988), Coupe de France (1980, 1985, 1991), Coppa delle Alpi (1979, 1983, 1984), Trophée des Champions (1985)

Managerial honours: Ligue 1 (2000), Trophée des Champions (2000), Coupe de la Ligue runner-up (2001)

Meet the New Boys

Nathan
REDMOND

FACTFILE:

Full name: Nathan Daniel Jerome Redmond

Date of birth: 6th March 1994

Place of birth: Birmingham, England

Height: 5ft 8in

Playing position: Winger

Former clubs: Birmingham City, Norwich City

Honours: Victory Shield (2009), Toulon Tournament (2016), Nordic Tournament (2010), Football League Championship play-off winner (2015)

1. Redmond has played at every youth level for England! The winger made his first appearance for his nation in 2009, as he represented the Three Lions at Under-16 level. Since then, Redmond has gone on to feature at Under-17, Under-18, Under-19, Under-20 and Under-21 level.

2. After joining Norwich City in 2013 from Birmingham City, Redmond scored his first goal for the Canaries against Southampton! The winger cut in from the left-hand side and fired home to earn his former club a 1-0 win.

3. Redmond is the second-youngest player to ever represent Birmingham City. When he came on against Rochdale in August 2010, Redmond was just 16 years and 173 days old – 34 days older than Trevor Francis was on his debut.

4. Redmond played with three Southampton players at the Toulon Tournament in the summer of 2016. James Ward-Prowse, Matt Targett and Jack Stephens were all part of Gareth Southgate's squad.

5. The winger is no stranger to the big occasion. Redmond scored in Norwich's Championship play-off semi-final success against Ipswich Town and again in the final against Middlesbrough.

Meet the New Boys

Pierre-Emile
HØJBJERG

FACTFILE:

Full name: Pierre-Emile Kordt Højbjerg

Date of birth: 5th August 1995

Place of birth: Copenhagen, Denmark

Height: 6ft 1in

Playing position: Midfielder

Former clubs: BK Skjold, FC Copenhagen, Brøndby IF, Bayern Munich II, Bayern Munich, FC Augsburg, Schalke 04

Honours: Bundesliga (2013, 2014), DFB-Pokal (2013, 2014), UEFA Champions League (2013), FIFA Club World Cup (2013), Danish Talent of the Year (2014)

1. At just 21 years old, Højbjerg is certainly a rising star in Danish football. He has 17 caps and one goal for the senior Denmark national team, having made his debut in May 2014. He has also played at every international level for Denmark from Under-16s upwards.

2. Højbjerg is the youngest player to have represented Bayern Munich in the Bundesliga. On 13th April 2013, the midfielder made his debut at the age of just 17 against 1. FC Nürnberg, coming on as a substitute. He went on to start the German Cup final win against Borussia Dortmund a season later.

3. His former manager at Bayern Munich, Pep Guardiola, is a big fan of the Danish international. The Spanish coach once compared Højbjerg's ability to that of Sergio Busquets for his technique on the ball and natural positioning on the pitch.

4. Højbjerg's versatility could prove very useful for Southampton. Although he is often deployed in the centre of midfield, he can play in both advanced and defensive positions, while he has also been known to contribute as a right wing-back on occasion.

5. According to Danish sports writer Søren Hanghøj, Højbjerg may soon be the biggest name from Denmark in the Premier League – exceeding the reputation of Tottenham's Christian Eriksen. Hanghøj said: "He's the player that the Danish national team is going to be built around for years to come. Eriksen is probably Denmark's star player right now, but Pierre-Emile is not far behind, that's for sure."

33

Meet the New Boys

Jérémy
PIED

FACTFILE:

Full name: Jérémy Pied

Date of birth: 23rd February 1989

Place of birth: Grenoble, France

Height: 5ft 8in

Playing position: Right-back

Former clubs: Lyon, Metz (loan), Nice, Guingamp (loan)

Honours: Coupe de France (2012)

1. Pied is linking up with Southampton manager Claude Puel for the third time in his career. The full-back has followed Puel from Lyon to Southampton, via Nice, who he played for regularly last season.

2. Pied was also a winner of the Coupe de France in 2012 with Lyon, after Puel departed the club. He helped Nice back into the Europa League last season, as they kept 13 clean sheets in Ligue 1 – the fifth meanest defence in the division.

3. Statistically speaking, Pied was highly rated in the French top-flight, with statistical website whoscored.com listing only two players – Djibril Sidibé, of Monaco, and Issiaga Sylla, of Toulouse – as having made more tackles and interceptions than Pied.

4. He graduated from a thriving academy, coming through the Olympique Lyonnais ranks at the same time as Alexandre Lacazette and Samuel Umtiti.

5. He becomes the first Frenchman to sign for Southampton since Dany N'Guessan. Although well served by Morgan Schneiderlin, Saints have not signed a French player since returning to the Premier League in 2012.

Meet the New Boys

Alex
McCarthy

FACTFILE:

Full name: Alex Simon McCarthy

Date of birth: 3rd December 1989

Place of birth: Guildford, England

Height: 6ft 4in

Playing position: Goalkeeper

Former clubs: Reading, Woking (loan), Cambridge United (loan), Team Bath (loan), Aldershot Town (loan), Yeovil Town (loan), Brentford (loan), Leeds United (loan), Ipswich Town (loan), QPR, Crystal Palace

1. McCarthy arrives at St Mary's with international experience already under his belt, having played three times for England Under-21s and making the senior squad in May 2013 for the first time.

2. The keeper created a unique record at an early age, playing in all of English football's top six divisions by the time he was just 22.

3. McCarthy played for 11 teams before joining Southampton – a journey that has taken in Team Bath in the Conference South, through to the Premier League with three other clubs. He was also considered for the Olympics, when he was named in the provisional Team GB squad of 35 players for London 2012.

4. McCarthy is already familiar with his new home at St Mary's, having played against Saints in a 1-1 draw for Ipswich Town in March 2012, while also visiting since then with QPR and his most recent club, Crystal Palace.

5. Statistically speaking, he impressed last season, with Arsenal's Petr Čech (78.3%) the only Premier League 'keeper to have made five or more appearances who had a better save success rate than McCarthy (76.2%).

Meet the New Boys

Sofiane
BOUFAL

FACTFILE:

Full name: Sofiane Boufal

Date of birth: 17th September 1993

Place of birth: Paris, France

Height: 5ft 9in

Playing position: Attacking midfielder

Former clubs: Angers, Lille

Honours: Marc-Vivien Foe Award 2016

1. Boufal won the Marc-Vivien Foe Award for the best African player in the French Ligue 1 at the end of the 2015/16 campaign. The Moroccan international became the fourth player from Lille to win the award since its inception in 2009, following on from Gervinho (2010 and 2011) and Vincent Enyeama (2014).

2. The attacking midfielder could have represented France, having been born in Paris, but he opted to represent Morocco at international level. He made his debut for Morocco in March 2016, starting a 1-0 victory against Cape Verde.

3. Boufal was handed his debut at the age of just 18. Playing for Angers, having progressed through their youth system, he came on in the closing stages of a 1-0 loss to FC Istres. His first start came a season later, this time in a 4-2 win against the same opponent.

4. The attacking midfielder has a real eye for goal. The 22 year-old finished the 2015/16 campaign as Lille's top scorer in all competitions, netting 11 in Ligue 1 and one in the Coupe de la Ligue.

5. Boufal becomes the fourth Moroccan to join Southampton. Hassan Kachloul was the first to become a Saint in 1998, before Tahar El Khalej joined in 2003. The last Moroccan to feature for the club was Youssef Safri, who joined in 2008.

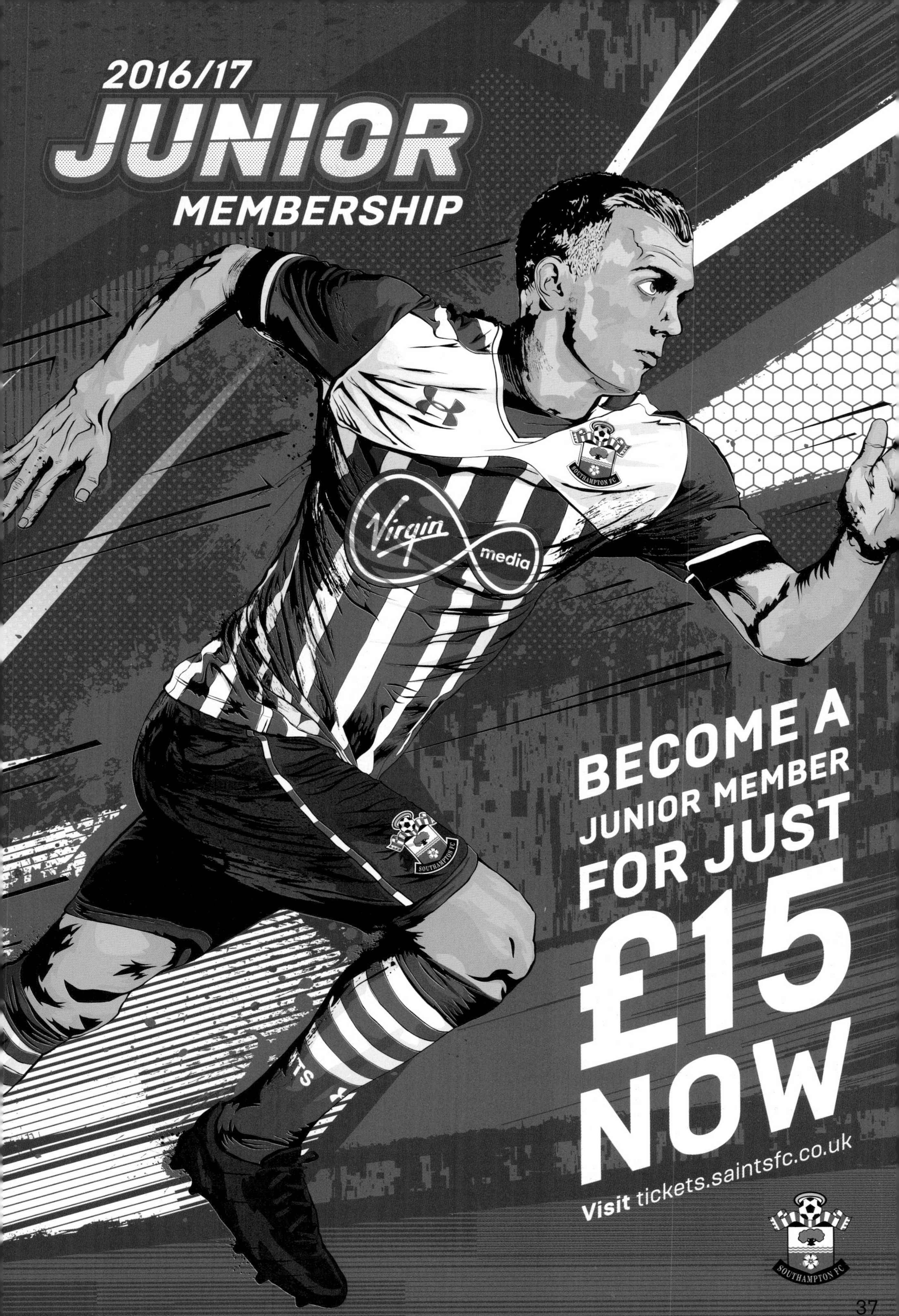
2016/17
JUNIOR
MEMBERSHIP
Virgin media
SOUTHAMPTON FC
BECOME A
JUNIOR MEMBER
FOR JUST
£15
NOW
Visit tickets.saintsfc.co.uk
SOUTHAMPTON FC

INSIDE THE SAINTS STORE

There are so many fantastic Southampton items in the Saints Stores! We've picked out nine great items that you can get your hands on either at St Mary's, WestQuay or online at store.saintsfc.co.uk!

HOME KIT | £40

WALL CLOCK | £12

SAMMY SAINT KEYRING | £14

SAINTS BEAKER | £7

SAINTS RUCKSACK | £14

BOXED STATIONERY SET | £8

SAINTS BELT | £7

A3 WALL STICKERS | £9

MASCOT SLIPPERS | £12

1 Fraser Forster

POSITION:	Goalkeeper
DATE OF BIRTH:	17th March 1988
JOINED SAINTS:	August 2014
PREVIOUS CLUBS:	Newcastle, Stockport (loan), Bristol Rovers (loan), Norwich (loan), Celtic
HEIGHT:	6ft 7in
NATIONALITY:	English

PROFILE

An enormous presence in goal, Forster has established himself as one of the Premier League's best keepers, while he is also a regular in the England squad. His run of 708 consecutive minutes without conceding a top-flight goal this season set a new club record.

Best moment of 2015/16: His astonishing display in the 0-0 draw at Arsenal, in February. Forster produced save after stunning save to keep the Gunners attack at bay, just a few weeks after returning from a ten-month lay-off with a knee injury.

2 Cédric

POSITION:	Right-back
DATE OF BIRTH:	31st August 1991
JOINED SAINTS:	June 2015
PREVIOUS CLUBS:	Sporting Club, Académica de Coimbra (loan)
HEIGHT:	5ft 8in
NATIONALITY:	Portuguese

PROFILE

An athletic right-back, Cédric is a well-established Portugal international and offers both a defensive and attacking side to his game. Impressive on the ball, he is a talented passer and is often a threat with his delivery from the right-hand side of the pitch when he gets forward.

Best moment of 2015/16: Cédric was superb in Southampton's memorable 3-1 win away to reigning champions Chelsea, in October. Defensively, he ended numerous Blues attacks, while he also played an important role in some of Saints' best counters.

3 Maya Yoshida

POSITION:	Centre-back
DATE OF BIRTH:	24th August 1988
JOINED SAINTS:	September 2012
PREVIOUS CLUBS:	Nagoya Grampus, VVV-Venlo
HEIGHT:	6ft 2in
NATIONALITY:	Japanese

PROFILE

The Japan international centre-back has often had to play the role of the chief back-up in his position, but has been a valued member of the squad since arriving. Now offering a more physical presence than when he first joined, Yoshida's cultured approach can also have a useful edge to it, while he is an under-rated goal threat.

Best moment of 2015/16: Yoshida chipped in with a couple of crucial goals, but his best one was surely the long-range, left-footed drive in the 2-1 home win over Aston Villa in the Capital One Cup, in October.

4 Jordy Clasie

POSITION:	Central midfield
DATE OF BIRTH:	27th June 1991
JOINED SAINTS:	July 2015
PREVIOUS CLUBS:	Excelsior, Feyenoord (loan)
HEIGHT:	5ft 7in
NATIONALITY:	Dutch

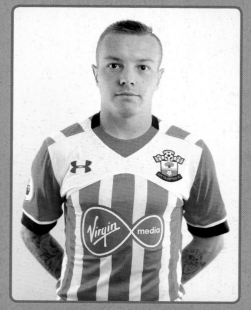

PROFILE

The Dutch international might be one of the shorter central midfielders around, but he certainly doesn't let that affect him. His tenacity in midfield makes him a strong defensive asset, while he is also a precise passer of the ball, capable of linking up play between the back and the front very effectively.

Best moment of 2015/16: A dominant midfield display in Southampton's 1-0 win away to Manchester United, in January. Clasie was an immense presence on what was a famous afternoon for Saints.

5 Florin Gardoș

POSITION: **Centre-back**
DATE OF BIRTH: **29th October 1988**
JOINED SAINTS: **August 2014**
PREVIOUS CLUBS: **Concordia Chiajna, Steaua Bucharest**
HEIGHT: **6ft 4in**
NATIONALITY: **Romanian**

PROFILE

Gardoș is an accomplished centre-half, who has been known throughout his career for his ability on the ball and his willingness to bring it forward and open up play from the back. Injuries have limited his involvement at the club, but the Romania international still has a bright future ahead of him.

Best moment of 2015/16: Gardoș missed the whole season with a knee injury, but his return to action in the under-21s' home victory over Norwich, in April, was a great moment for him and all those watching.

6 José Fonte

POSITION: **Centre-back**
DATE OF BIRTH: **22nd December 1983**
JOINED SAINTS: **January 2010**
PREVIOUS CLUBS: **Sporting Club, SC Salgueiros, FC Felgueiras, Vitória Setúbal, Benfica, Paços Ferreira (loan), Estrela Amadora (loan), Crystal Palace**
HEIGHT: **6ft 2in**
NATIONALITY: **Portuguese**

PROFILE

Fonte has been with Saints ever since League 1, becoming team captain in 2014. The Portugal international has been a rock at the back ever since joining. He is capable of mixing it physically with any striker in the league, but is also extremely impressive on the ball, with a good passing range. It is not uncommon for him to chip in with a goal, either.

Best moment of 2015/16: Maybe not his best individual moment, but one of the proudest was surely leading Southampton to a 3-0 home Europa League win over Vitesse in July 2015 – the club's first European win in 34 years.

7 Shane Long

POSITION:	Striker
DATE OF BIRTH:	22nd January 1987
JOINED SAINTS:	August 2014
PREVIOUS CLUBS:	Cork City, Reading, West Bromwich Albion, Hull City
HEIGHT:	5ft 11in
NATIONALITY:	Irish

PROFILE

A talented hurler and musician, but an even better footballer. Long's pace and relentless running make him a thorn in the side for many defenders. He also offers an incredible leap, making him a huge threat in the air. Has played out wide at times for Saints, but has been at his best when used as a central striker.

Best moment of 2015/16: Plenty of options, but his goal and two assists in a must-win encounter at Aston Villa in April helped give Saints a 4-2 victory and push them towards Europe.

8 Steven Davis

POSITION:	Central/right midfield
DATE OF BIRTH:	1st January 1985
JOINED SAINTS:	July 2012
PREVIOUS CLUBS:	Aston Villa, Fulham, Rangers
HEIGHT:	5ft 8in
NATIONALITY:	Northern Irish

PROFILE

Davis has been one of Southampton's most dependable players since his arrival. His link-up play is superb, with his creativity perhaps one of the more under-rated aspects of his game. He has increasingly become a goal threat, and can really play anywhere in midfield, from a deep lying role, to a position on the right, to perhaps his best spot in an advanced area.

Best moment of 2015/16: His double away to Tottenham in the penultimate game of the season, which saw Saints come from behind to win 2-1 and take a huge step towards European qualification.

9 Jay Rodriguez

POSITION:	Striker
DATE OF BIRTH:	29th July 1989
JOINED SAINTS:	June 2012
PREVIOUS CLUBS:	Burnley, Stirling Albion (loan), Barnsley (loan)
HEIGHT:	6ft 1in
NATIONALITY:	English

PROFILE

A rapid forward, who combines his speed with a devastating finishing ability. Rodriguez, who has earned England recognition since joining Saints, is unplayable when at his best and, although injuries have held him back a bit recently, he remains a huge goal threat when in the team.

Best moment of 2015/16: His stunning goal in the 6-0 Capital One Cup win over MK Dons, in September, as Rodriguez broke from the halfway line before curling in a wonderful shot from 18 yards.

10 Charlie Austin

POSITION:	Striker
DATE OF BIRTH:	5th July 1989
JOINED SAINTS:	January 2016
PREVIOUS CLUBS:	Kintbury Rangers, Hungerford Town, Poole Town, Swindon Town, Burnley, QPR
HEIGHT:	6ft 2in
NATIONALITY:	English

PROFILE

Austin is a prolific striker, who has risen all the way from non-league to the top level of the English game. As good a finisher as they come, the forward is a predatory marksman, while also possessing the capacity for some quite sensational goals.

Best moment of 2015/16: It doesn't get much better than coming off the bench at Old Trafford and scoring the winner against Manchester United on your debut, as Austin did in January.

11 Dušan Tadić

POSITION: **Central midfield/winger**
DATE OF BIRTH: **20th November 1988**
JOINED SAINTS: **July 2014**
PREVIOUS CLUBS: **FK Vojvodina, FC Groningen, FC Twente**
HEIGHT: **5ft 11in**
NATIONALITY: **Serbian**

PROFILE

Tadić is one of the Premier League's most creative players, consistently ranking near the top of the assist charts. His skill, balance and poise make him a joy to watch and a nightmare for defenders. Capable of playing on either flank, he is also a threat when used through the middle, behind the strikers.

Best moment of 2015/16: His triple-assist effort in the 4-2 home win over Manchester City, in May. Tadić set up two for Sadio Mané and one for Shane Long, on his way to 13 assists for the season.

14 Oriol Romeu

POSITION: **Central midfield**
DATE OF BIRTH: **24th September 1991**
JOINED SAINTS: **August 2015**
PREVIOUS CLUBS: **Barcelona, Chelsea, Valencia (loan), VfB Stuttgart (loan)**
HEIGHT: **6ft 0in**
NATIONALITY: **Spanish**

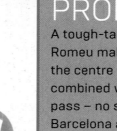

PROFILE

A tough-tackling defensive midfield player, Romeu makes for a significant presence in the centre of the pitch. His physicality is well combined with an ease on the ball and eye for a pass – no surprise given he came through the Barcelona academy – while he has also provided a few foals.

Best moment of 2015/16: His late equaliser in a 1-1 home draw against Aston Villa, in December. Not the best result on the face of it at the time, but it proved to be a big point come the end of the season.

15 Cuco Martina

POSITION:	Right-back
DATE OF BIRTH:	25th September 1989
JOINED SAINTS:	July 2015
PREVIOUS CLUBS:	RBC Roosendaal, RKC Waalwijk, FC Twente
HEIGHT:	6ft 1in
NATIONALITY:	Curaçaoan

PROFILE

A quick and athletic full-back, Martina is an all-action performer who enjoyed a memorable first season at Southampton. The Curaçao captain was a regular in the team by the end of the campaign, with his speed making him a strong asset, while he also offers a threat in the attacking third.

Best moment of 2015/16: Martina's wonder strike in the 4-0 home win over Arsenal was undoubtedly Saints' best goal of the season and, without question, his most memorable moment.

16 James Ward-Prowse

POSITION:	Central/right midfield
DATE OF BIRTH:	1st November 1994
JOINED SAINTS:	Academy graduate
PREVIOUS CLUBS:	None
HEIGHT:	5ft 8in
NATIONALITY:	English

PROFILE

The England Under-21 captain is one of the most promising central midfield players in the country, but already backs that up with significant experience, having made more than 100 career first-team appearances. A brilliant passer and also a notable dead-ball specialist.

Best moment of 2015/16: His stunning free-kick that set Saints on the way to a 3-0 home win over West Brom in January, finding the top corner from 25 yards, before also scoring a penalty in the same game.

17 Virgil van Dijk

POSITION:	Centre-back
DATE OF BIRTH:	8th July 1991
PREVIOUS CLUBS:	FC Groningen, Celtic
HEIGHT:	6ft 4in
NATIONALITY:	Dutch

PROFILE

Van Dijk has all the tools you could want from a centre-back, quickly establishing himself as one of the Premier League's best. Tall, strong and powerful, he also possesses a speed that can help avert danger, while his ability on the ball is incredibly impressive. Unsurprisingly, with those skills, he can be a potent force in the opposition penalty area as well.

Best moment of 2015/16: His clean-sweep of the Player of the Season prizes. Van Dijk was selected by both his teammates and the Saints supporters as the side's most outstanding performer during the campaign.

18 Harrison Reed

POSITION:	Central midfield
DATE OF BIRTH:	27th January 1995
JOINED SAINTS:	Academy graduate
PREVIOUS CLUBS:	None
HEIGHT:	5ft 9in
NATIONALITY:	English

PROFILE

A tenacious defensive midfield player, Reed is a regular with the under-21s, but has shown significant promise when he has been called up to the first-team. Reed is a strong-willed competitor, who is comfortable on the ball and has an impressive strike on him as well. Certainly one to watch in the next few years.

Best moment of 2015/16: First-team appearances were limited for Reed during the season, but he was involved in both wins over Vitesse in the Europa League third qualifying round tie.

21 Ryan Bertrand

POSITION:	Left-back
DATE OF BIRTH:	5th August 1989
JOINED SAINTS:	July 2014
PREVIOUS CLUBS:	Chelsea, Bournemouth (loan), Oldham Athletic (loan), Norwich City (loan), Reading (loan), Nottingham Forest (loan), Aston Villa (loan)
HEIGHT:	5ft 10in
NATIONALITY:	English

PROFILE

After a number of loan spells around the country, Bertrand finally found a permanent home in Southampton, following an initial temporary spell, and has since blossomed into one of the Premier League's best full-backs. A regular with England, he is versatile enough to play as a left-sided centre-back, while he possesses a threatening delivery, coupled with a stern defensive resilience.

Best moment of 2015/16: His emphatic penalty kick in the final game of the season, at home to Crystal Palace, helped to seal a 4-1 victory that ensured Saints went marching back into Europe.

33 Matt Targett

POSITION:	Left-back
DATE OF BIRTH:	18th September 1995
JOINED SAINTS:	Academy graduate
PREVIOUS CLUBS:	None
HEIGHT:	6ft 0in
NATIONALITY:	English

PROFILE

An England Under-21 international, who has made impressive strides since coming through the Saints academy. Targett possesses a great deal of potential and has been a strong understudy to Ryan Bertrand at left-back. His left foot can be a real threat from deep, while he is known for his committed displays in defence.

Best moment of 2015/16: Voted by supporters as the club's Player of the Month for January. His pin-point cross for Shane Long in the 2-0 win over Watford that ended a dreadful run of form was crucial in the season.

TEAMMATES

WITH JAMES WARD-PROWSE

Want to get the inside track on the Saints players? So do we! With that in mind, we caught up with midfielder James Ward-Prowse to get the scoop on his teammates.

Who is the best trainer?

I think José Fonte takes that prize. He's the captain and he sets a really good example for all the other lads with the way he approaches training. He's very professional about it and always takes it seriously.

Who is the most skilful?

I'd probably have to say Nathan Redmond, now that he's come into the club. He'd definitely be up there. He's got a lot of ability on the ball, and one-v-one with a player, he can give a full-back a really torrid time, which he'll hopefully do for us now.

Who is the biggest joker?

I can't say Kelvin Davis anymore, can I?! He'd definitely have won

this one! I'd probably have to say Charlie Austin now. He's always got a bit of banter about him and is having a joke with people – nothing too bad, though!

Who is the funniest?

For me, I would say Maya Yoshida. He's a lovely guy, but he does some funny stuff sometimes. It's hard to explain, but you just think 'Ah, that's Maya!'

Who is the most intelligent?

Fraser Forster. He's quiet, but you can tell he's got a good intellectual background. He knows a

lot of stuff and he got very good exam results. He went to a good school as well, so he's definitely got a bit about him in that sense.

Who has the best dress sense?

There's a couple to be fair. José and Cédric think they've got a bit, but I think I'd probably go with Jay. He's got a nice range of attire, which is similar to the sort of stuff that I like.

Who has the worst dress sense?

Matty Targett! A few of the lads got onto him about it last year. It's just that the jeans don't fit him right. He needs some better jeans and then I think he'll be alright.

Who is the hardest man?

I'd go Oriol Romeu. I think he's related to the King in the North in Game of Thrones. He's a wild one! He's a lovely guy, but he kicks people! You certainly wouldn't want to mess with him. I'm just glad we're on the same team.

Who is the best dancer?

Now this one has to go to Nathan Redmond. He's got some very nice moves when he gets out there on the floor.

Who is the worst dancer?

There's a lot more competition for this one. I'd struggle to pick just one person, as we've got so many bad ones!

Hardest shot?

Virgil van Dijk. He has got an absolute hammer foot. He absolutely swings it and then bang! Fortunately, I've never got in the way of one of them, but the 'keepers definitely say he's got the hardest shot.

Best taste in music?

José! He's in charge of the iPod in the changing room. He's got a mix – a bit of Spanish, Portuguese, RnB and house, so he's got all the lads on-side I think.

Worst taste in music?

That is Virgil, without a shadow of a doubt. He's forever bringing out terrible Dutch songs that no one has ever heard of. It's awful, so he's definitely the worst in that sense.

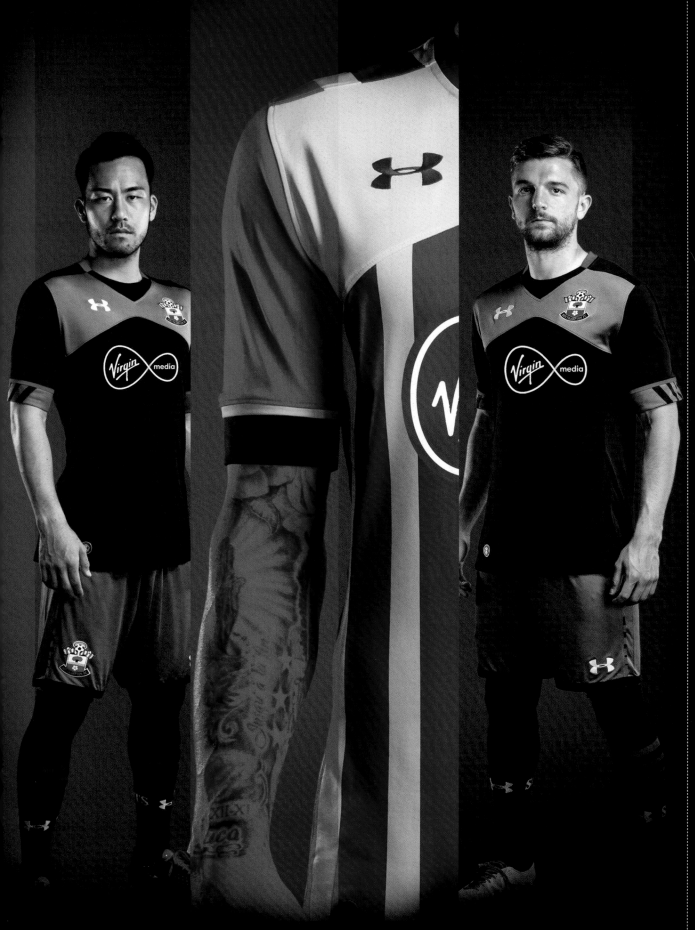

FOOD FOR FOOTBALL

Have you ever wanted to play like your favourite Saints star? Well, one of the most important steps along the way is making sure you eat like they do.

FOOTBALLERS' diets are a hugely important part of their performance on the pitch, and you can improve your own game by making sure you take on board the right food and drink.

To find out what's best for you, we spoke to Southampton's Performance Chef, Tom Kenton.

"The whole idea is that the food is the fuel for the player's body," he said. "It's like putting fuel into your car. If you don't have it, you don't go anywhere, and if you put the wrong type of fuel in, it doesn't work either.

"The main thing is that it's easily digestible foods – like chicken, which is high in protein – so your body's not working to break down the food. It can concentrate on using the energy to perform.

"Certain days you would need to eat more carbohydrates than other days, depending on your training schedule. Obviously, if you know you've got PE on a Tuesday, then you can start increasing the amount of carbs you are eating on Sunday night and Monday, ready for the big day on the Tuesday.

"We talk about matchday minus-one and minus-two, which are our fuelling days. Just remember whatever you eat on those two days before is your fuel for that game.

"When it comes to the pre-match meal, that's not actually designed to fuel you, but for your comfort in the game. Some people might eat more, some people might eat less, but it's not what they eat then that's getting them through the game – it's what they've done in the two days before that. Just make sure you're not bloated or full up.

"After your matchday, you want to eat some high protein food – e.g. red meat – to boost your blood cells for your recovery – things like plenty of beetroot – then you're working again towards matchday."

Tom and nutritionist Mike Naylor have put together their top-five foods and snacks, as well as a daily meal plan for you to follow.

Tom added: "The top-five foods are quite easy to fit into your meal plan, but in a different way. The majority of my job is doing what is, in essence, the same food, but making it different each day.

"The players are eating chicken every day, so it's a case of how can you make it different, and you actually find that you can make chicken dishes from all over the globe.

"If you get used to clean eating then you enjoy it. Some of the guys here really do love eating boiled vegetables! It's just getting the right nutrients into your body."

TOP-FIVE FOODS TO EAT/DRINK:

Eating a variety of all of these is a must for every footballer:

BROCCOLI
High in vitamins and minerals to support immune heath and energy for players.

CHICKEN
A lean source of protein to support muscle recovery.

PASTA
Carbohydrate-rich food, which is perfect for maximising muscle glycogen – a primary fuel for matchday performance.

BEETROOT
High in dietary nitrates, which help oxygen delivery to muscles, improving endurance.

MILK
A great source of calcium and protein, supporting muscle development and recovery from tough training sessions.

TOP-FIVE SNACKS:

FRUIT
It is a good idea to eat the full colour of the rainbow, which will help you to get a full set of vitamins and minerals.

GREEK YOGURT
This is a high-protein and low-sugar snack, which supports muscle development and recovery.

NUTS & SEEDS
These might be high in fat, but they are good fats that

your body requires.

BEEF JERKY
A lot of people wouldn't think of this, but it's a great source of protein.

CRUDITÉS & LOW-FAT HUMMUS
Crudités – raw vegetables – go very well with the hummus, and this gives you a wide range of vitamins and minerals.

A DAY'S MENU FOR A FOOTBALLER

Find out how to eat like a Saints player for an entire day! At the end of each dish, we've included the beneficial contents.

BREAKFAST
Three eggs, either scrambled or poached, on wholegrain toast with spinach on the side and two pieces of fruit (carbs, protein, vitamins and minerals).

MID-MORNING SNACK
Greek yogurt with mixed berries (protein & vitamins).

LUNCH
Grilled Cajun chicken, dry-baked potato wedges, broccoli, carrots & green beans with homemade tomato relish, and with a piece of fruit to finish (a balanced meal, high in protein, carbs, vitamins and minerals, as well as low fat).

AFTERNOON SNACK
Beef jerky (high protein snack to keep you full for the afternoon).

DINNER
Baked salmon, a warm quinoa salad and roasted Mediterranean vegetables (another balanced meal, very colourful and high in vitamins, minerals and protein, while lower in carbs).

Yogurt and berries for dessert (protein and vitamins).

EVENING SNACK
A glass of milk and a piece of fruit (high calcium and protein).

Remember that your portion size should reflect the amount of exercise you do, so increase or decrease it accordingly. Just remember your food is your fuel, so think how much you need to put into your body for the games or training sessions that you've got coming up, or how much you need to refuel after finishing your work.

THE SCIENCE BEHIND SUCCESS

Want to know how the Saints players perform so well on the pitch? Well, it isn't just the work they do over 90 minutes that counts.

How they prepare for their matches and how they recover from them is also vitally important – and it can help your own game too!

To find out how you can get an edge, we spoke to Southampton's Head of Sports Science, Alek Gross.

How do Saints warm-up properly?

"The basic principle is abbreviated to RAMP – so, we Raise, Activate, Mobilise and Potentiate," explained Alek.

"When it comes to raising heart rate, you're talking about any activity that will increase the circulation and increase the blood flow to the working muscles. So, on a match day you'll see some of the initial warm-up activities are around jogging and football-based activities. That's just to raise heart rate.

"We also activate, so the key muscles are mobilised. Some of the stuff people will have seen in pre-season, where the boys are on mats or using bands, that's to activate the muscles that are required for playing – particularly the lower body muscles that generate speed and power, while it's also for injury prevention as well as performance. By doing that, we are also mobilising the joints that are involved as well.

"The last bit is potentiate. That's where we're looking at generating speed. So the last part of the warm-up is generally around fast feet and acceleration. It's also where we introduce the football-based movements, so some of the finishing drills that the forwards will do is also based around the movements that they do at game pace, and also the possession and keep-ball that we do is around that as well."

What's some good advice for our readers when warming up?

"The key one is sleeping the night before. Your performance starts by making sure you sleep well before, and also getting adequate food and hydration in the morning.

"When it comes to before the match, it's a bit old fashioned, but jogging round the pitch will raise heart rate and it's very similar to what we do.

"Also do some basic stretches around the key muscle groups, and make sure you do kick a ball before you start. It's also a good idea to then do some fast movements and some sprints.

"There's also the FIFA 11+ standardised warm-up that you can easily access on the internet, and our academy have been associated with that in developing it for kids. It's a simple warm-up that anyone can do. You don't need any specialist knowledge or equipment, you can just follow 11 pretty simple instructions."

How important is it to warm up properly?

"Ultimately, if you don't warm up you're not going to perform that well. Especially in the winter where it's cold, it's more important and you might have to elongate that warm-up.

"It's also important to get mentally ready and to get a few touches on the football to allow you to perform better, while it plays a big part in injury prevention – the last thing any child needs is not playing, and the risk of getting injured if you don't warm up properly is severely increased."

What are the key principles in recovering from a match?

"Pretty simple pillars of recovery are eat right, sleep right and train right in between, so our first port of call post-match is hydration – making sure people drink an adequate amount of water.

"Replenishing by half a litre or a litre of water until you're no longer thirsty is pretty important and a pretty simple way of approaching it.

"Also, you want to get in some food as soon as you can. Ideally eat a well-balanced meal within 60 minutes of finishing – something that has a bit of protein, carbohydrate, fruit and veg in there.

"The next thing is making sure you get at least eight hours sleep, and not looking at your phone or iPad immediately before bed, because not only will it delay you going to sleep, but it also means you won't get the same quality of deep sleep you want.

"You also then need to make sure that you train adequately in the week, which includes warm-ups. If you're not warming-up properly in the week then that will affect your ability to recover. After that is when micro-strategies, such as ice baths and compression garments come in, but generally eating right and sleeping right will go a long way."

How important is recovering properly?

"For the first-team players, it's vital in terms of playing three games a week, or even two games a week – the ability to recover quickly and to be able to train as quickly as you can after it, to maintain performance levels is really important, but that drops down to anyone playing the sport.

"That's especially true for anyone who might be playing two games for a club or school, and they're doing PE and everything else in between.

"If they're not resting right, eating right and sleeping right in between they will potentially get injured, their general health won't be as good, they'll probably get ill a bit more, so making sure you look after yourself in between bouts of activities is very important."

PREMIER LEAGUE FOCUS

We take a look at the key players you need to watch out for on the opposing teams at St Mary's over the course of the 2016/17 campaign.

AFC BOURNEMOUTH

After missing much of the 2015/16 season with injury, Callum Wilson will be looking to make his mark for the Cherries this campaign. The striker scored 28 goals in 63 appearances during his first two seasons at Dean Court.

CRYSTAL PALACE

Midfielder Yohan Cabaye has the experience that will be key for Alan Pardew's Palace in 2016/17. Having featured for Newcastle United and PSG, the French international netted six times in 40 games last season.

ARSENAL

Winger Alexis Sanchez is the main man for the Gunners. The former Barcelona man, who now wears the number seven shirt, scored 42 goals in his first two seasons at Emirates Stadium. He also scored two against Saints during the 2014/15 campaign.

EVERTON

Attacking midfielder Ross Barkley will be looking to thrive under Ronald Koeman. The Englishman featured in every league game last season, scoring eight goals – including one against Saints.

BURNLEY

Striker Andre Gray was one of the main reasons why Burnley won promotion from the Championship last season. After joining from Brentford, he netted an impressive 25 times in 44 games to help the Clarets back to the top flight.

HULL CITY

Back from a long-term injury, Robert Snodgrass will be looking to make his mark in the Premier League. The former Leeds United and Norwich City man scored on the opening day of the new season against Leicester City, and bagged 12 in the top-flight with the Canaries between 2012 and 2014.

CHELSEA

It was a disappointing season for Eden Hazard during 2015/16, but the Belgian winger will be a key man for Antonio Conte's Chelsea this time around. Hazard, who won PFA Player of the Year in 2015, has scored 55 goals in 205 games for the Blues.

LEICESTER CITY

Jamie Vardy was linked with a big-money move to Arsenal in the summer, but the England man stayed with the champions. The striker scored an impressive 24 goals in the Premier League during the 2015/16 campaign.

LIVERPOOL

A former Saint, Sadio Mané will be looking to impress for Liverpool following his big-money move in the summer. Mané scored 15 goals in all competitions for Saints last season, including a hat-trick against Manchester City.

MANCHESTER CITY

A two-time Premier League winner, Sergio Agüero has been an important part of Manchester City's side since joining in 2011. Last season, the Argentine striker netted 29 times in 44 matches.

MANCHESTER UNITED

Anthony Martial had an excellent first season in the Premier League. The French international scored 17 goals in 49 appearances in all competitions, lifting silverware in his first season as the Red Devils won the FA Cup.

MIDDLESBROUGH

A big-name signing for Boro, Álvaro Negredo has a point to prove in the Premier League. Formerly of Manchester City, the striker returns to England following a spell with Valencia. Along with former Saints Gastón Ramírez, the 31 year-old will be a key man for Boro.

STOKE CITY

After a season of settling in to the Premier League, Xherdan Shaqiri will be key for Stoke City. The Swiss international, who has played for Bayern Munich and Inter Milan, scored three goals last season – including a great strike at Everton.

SUNDERLAND

Having signed a new deal in the summer, Jermain Defoe will once again be the man Sunderland looks to for goals. He scored 15 times in the Premier League last season to ensure the Black Cats of their survival for another year.

SWANSEA CITY

Iceland international Gylfi Sigurdsson is Swansea's key man. The attacking midfielder scored 11 goals in 33 games last season, including a number of excellent free-kicks.

TOTTENHAM HOTSPUR

England striker Harry Kane will be looking to continue his excellent form over the last two seasons. The Spurs man netted an impressive 59 goals during 2014/15 and 2015/16, and will be leading the line for Mauricio Pochettino's side again.

WATFORD

Striker Odion Ighalo had an excellent debut season in the Premier League last time around. The 27-year-old netted 15 goals for the Hornets, who finished 14th in the table.

WEST BROMWICH ALBION

Having had one season to adjust, Salomón Rondón will be hoping for a big season with the Baggies. The Venezuela striker scored ten goals in his 40 appearances during his first year in England.

WEST HAM UNITED

Dimitri Payet certainly made an impression for the Hammers during his first season in England. The Frenchman scored 12 goals in 38 appearances during 2015/16, with his stunning free-kicks a key aspect of his game.

THE BIG QUIZ

1. Who finished the 2015/16 season as Southampton's top scorer in all competitions?

2. Who did Southampton win their first league game of the 2015/16 season against?

3. How many points did Southampton pick up in the Premier League in 2015/16?

4. How many consecutive minutes did Fraser Forster go without conceding a goal during January and February 2016?

5. Who won the Players' Player and Fans' Player awards at the end of season dinner?

6. Who scored the club's 2015/16 Goal of the Season?

7. Who was rewarded with a testimonial match for his ten years of service to Southampton?

8. Who scored the club's first goal of the 2015/16 campaign in all competitions?

9. Against which team did James Ward-Prowse score his two goals during the 2015/16 campaign?

10. Can you name the two Saints players who represented England at EURO 2016 in the summer?

11. Southampton won two games in a row 4-2 towards the end of the 2015/16 season. Can you name the two teams they beat?

12. Who was the scorer of Saints' only hat-trick last season?

13. Which player went out on loan to Barnsley and won two matches at Wembley?

14. No team beat Southampton in both league matches last season. True or false?

15. Can you name which player grabbed 13 assists for Southampton during 2015/16?

16. Against which team did Southampton record their biggest win of the season against in all competitions?

17. Who scored the goals when Southampton beat AFC Bournemouth 2-0 in the first Premier League meeting between the two sides?

18. Who did Southampton beat in the third qualifying round of the UEFA Europa League?

19. Who made the most appearances in the Premier League last season?

20. Which player scored Southampton's only FA Cup goal in 2015/16?

THE NUMBERS GAME

1. Who wears the number 16 shirt for Southampton?

2. If you add up Oriol Romeu and Cédric's squad numbers, what figure do you have?

3. José Fonte wears what number shirt for Southampton?

4. Which goalkeeper has the highest squad number for Southampton?

5. If you add Steven Davis, Shane Long and Jay Rodriguez's squad numbers together, what figure do you now have?

WHO AM I?

1. I joined from Crystal Palace when the club was in League 1 and have now gone on to become captain of Southampton. Who am I?

2. I am the captain of my country and wear the number eight shirt for Southampton. Who am I?

3. I won two awards in my first season with Southampton after joining from Scottish side Celtic. Who am I?

4. I have won the UEFA Champions League and previously had a loan spell at AFC Bournemouth. Who am I?

5. I scored my first goal for Southampton in a Capital One Cup match against Stoke City during the 2014/15 season. Who am I?

Answers on page 62/63.

SPOT THE SAINTS

We've hidden five Saints players in the crowd at St Mary's.
Can you spot them all?

Quiz & Puzzle ANSWERS

WORD**SEARCH**

ANSWERS to page 49.

CROSS**WORD**

ANSWERS to page 49.

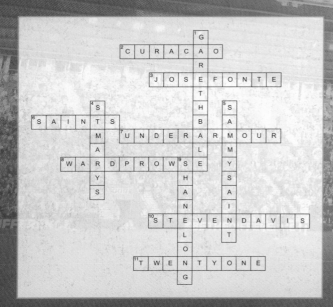

THE **BIG** QUIZ

ANSWERS to page 58.

1. Sadio Mané

2. Norwich City

3. 63

4. 708 minutes

5. Virgil van Dijk

6. Cuco Martina vs Arsenal (H)

7. Kelvin Davis

8. Graziano Pellè vs Vitesse

9. West Bromwich Albion

10. Ryan Bertrand and Fraser Forster

11. Aston Villa and Manchester City

12. Sadio Mané

13. Lloyd Isgrove

14. True

15. Dušan Tadić

16. MK Dons (6-0 in the Capital One Cup)

17. Steven Davis and Graziano Pellè

18. Vitesse

19. José Fonte

20. Oriol Romeu